JAMES JOYCE

A Life from Beginning to End

Table of Contents

Introduction

Few figures in Irish history are as well-known as James Joyce. He was born into hardship in a country mired in political conflict, but rather than allow himself to get bogged down, he used his experiences to revolutionize the art of literature. His work, in his time, was both subversive and controversial. On the one hand, it made publication difficult, which contributed to Joyce spending the majority of his life in poverty. On the other, the politics surrounding the publication of his work led to free publicity and broader public interest, which eventually led him to success.

James Joyce did not achieve all this alone; his life was replete with colleagues, friends, and fellow artists who supported him financially, encouraged him to keep writing, and even self-published his books in spite of the potential legal consequences. People believed in James Joyce, and thanks to their unflinching aid, we are today blessed with some of the most well-regarded modernist literature ever written.

Chapter One

An Artist is Born

"Children must be educated by love, not punishment."

—James Joyce

James Augustine Joyce was born on February 2, 1882, in Dublin, Ireland, to parents John and May. Of their ten surviving children, James was the eldest. Like his six sisters and three brothers after him, he was baptized a few days after his birth into the Roman Catholic Church, as was the custom and expectation at the time.

The Joyces were a relatively well-to-do family with a long history of entrepreneurial success throughout Ireland. John's side of the family owned a salt and lime works in County Cork, and his father (James's grandfather) had married the daughter of a prominent Cork politician who also owned a drapery business and several properties throughout the city of Cork.

In 1887, John became a rate collector for the Dublin Corporation. A rate collector was, in essence, a debt collector—his duties would have included collecting weekly interest on loans or mortgages, as well as collecting fees for city services such as power, gas, and other utilities. While it was not a well-loved position in the public eye, it was well-paid, which allowed the Joyce family to move to the up-and-coming town of Bray, a few miles outside Dublin. This prosperity would not last long for the Joyces, however, as in just a few years, serious financial troubles would come knocking at their door.

Young James developed several unique phobias during these early years of his childhood, including a fear of dogs after a neighbor's dog bit him and a fear of thunderstorms. His uneasiness around storms was attributed to a superstitious aunt, who used to tell Joyce that the thunder was a sign of God's wrath. To a young boy from a staunchly Roman Catholic family, this would have been frightening indeed.

At seven years old, James was then sent off to Clongowes Wood College near Clane, County Kildare. Attending a boarding school was normal at the time and expected of the eldest sons of the family. It was, in essence, the beginning of

Joyce's education, and he would excel during his time there. Here, in 1891, a nine-year-old James Joyce produced his first piece of published writing—a poem titled "Et Tu, Healy," which he penned upon the death of Charles Stewart Parnell. His father had it printed and distributed to friends and family; he even sent a copy to the Pope.

Parnell had been a prominent Irish political figure during this period in history and had led the Home Rule Party, whose primary goal was to establish the independent sovereignty of Ireland from the United Kingdom. This was a contentious issue at the time, with violence becoming more and more common on both sides. Parnell made friends of the Fenian activist groups as well as the Irish Republican Brotherhood (a precursor to the later IRA, or Irish Republican Army) and helped further their goals by engaging in political action—most often obstruction of legislation that would prosecute such groups or lead the Irish government away from demanding and establishing independence.

Unfortunately, a personal scandal in Parnell's life would cause significant controversy in both the Irish and British Parliaments. It is unclear how the information came to light, but it was revealed that Parnell had been engaged in an extramarital affair for years, which led the Home Rule Party to split, with a majority aligning themselves separate from Parnell. Many British liberals, upset by the revelation, also distanced themselves from Parnell. The scandal was further exacerbated by the fact many Catholic bishops publicly denounced him for the affair, in essence ending his political career.

The poem that Joyce wrote upon Parnell's death largely echoed the opinions of his father, John, who felt that the Home Rule Party, the British liberals, and the Catholic Church itself had betrayed Parnell, and that was the reason the Irish failed to secure home rule in the British Parliament. These sentiments would have a profound effect on the young James Joyce as he got older, and many of these emotions and ideas would become apparent throughout his work.

At any rate, it was the same year, in 1891, that the Joyce family fortunes would take a turn for the worse. This sudden shift into poverty was a paradox of gradual and all at once, as it was a result of Joyce's father mismanaging the family finances, as well as his worsening drinking problem. By the end of that year, John Joyce's name was listed in *Stubbs' Gazette*, which had a list of local debtors and those who were bankrupt, essentially making it impossible for them to borrow from any other institutions. This also had personal ramifications, as after John's name was published in the *Gazette*, he was suspended from work. John's temporary suspension then became permanent in January of 1893 when he was dismissed from his position. James had to leave his boarding school around the same time, since his father could no longer pay the fees.

With James now back at home, he continued to study on his own. He attended the Christian Brothers O'Connell School in Dublin for a short time, but funds were too tight in the family to justify a continued enrollment. Then, a bit of luck for the young Joyce came in the form of his father having a random encounter with a Jesuit priest who tangentially knew the family and their struggles. John Conmee, the priest, arranged for James and his brother Stanislaus to attend Belvedere College in Dublin on full scholarships beginning in 1893.

James thrived once he was back in an educational environment. At the age of 13, he was elected by his classmates to join the Sodality of Our Lady. This was a religious brotherhood for young boys who devoted themselves to attending Mass daily, confession weekly, communion monthly, and meditating daily for at least a half-hour. In addition to this, the brotherhood would perform charitable works. To join the Sodality of Our Lady was a great honor at the time, and Joyce's membership would also influence his later writing.

Joyce graduated in 1898 after five years at Belvedere College. In his final two years before graduating, he won first place for English composition, perhaps a preview of the literary success that would come in the following years of his life.

Chapter Two

Forming Bonds and Forming Ideas

"All things are inconstant except the faith in the soul, which changes all things and fills their inconstancy with light."

—James Joyce

Following his graduation from Belvedere College, Joyce attended University College in Dublin with a focus on English, French, and Italian. He particularly enjoyed the works of Thomas Aquinas, which he was introduced to during his university studies. The writings of Aquinas would have a profound effect on Joyce's personal worldview and, subsequently, his professional works.

Thomas Aquinas, a medieval Italian priest of the Dominican Order, was one of the earliest proponents of natural theology—the idea that logic, reason, and even science could be used to prove the existence of a divine entity such as God. This view differs from most other theological arguments that depend on the scripture or other religious texts, or *a priori* from general life experiences. Unlike other philosophers and theologists of the Catholic Church in Aquinas' time, he admired and drew heavily from Aristotle and dedicated a large portion of his writing to marrying Aristotle's principles with those of Christianity as a whole. He also wrote extensively on metaphysics, ethics, and politics, and his writing is the basis of much of our modern-day philosophical schools of thought.

While at University College, Joyce became heavily involved in Dublin's literary circles and theatrical community. He became close friends with several individuals who would later become influential figures of their generation in Ireland. These included Tom Kettle, a politician and poet who injected new life into the Irish Parliamentary Party after Parnell's departure. He was a gifted speaker, and Joyce considered him to be his best friend while at school. Kettle was later killed in action on the Western Front during World War I.

Another was Oliver St. John Gogarty, who would later serve as the basis for the character

Buck Mulligan in Joyce's masterpiece *Ulysses*. Gogarty was a published poet and infamous prankster, and during the Irish War of Independence, he had a key role in the movement of IRA volunteers. Later, as a politician, he advocated staunchly for improved housing and school health services.

Francis Sheehy Skeffington was another close friend of Joyce's in his university days and was the model for the character MacCann in Joyce's later work *A Portrait of the Artist as a Young Man*. Skeffington and his wife were leaders in the women's suffrage movement in Ireland, and they both supported Irish home rule. Skeffington would later be killed during the Easter Rising of 1916 (an armed insurrection by the Irish to oust British rule).

These colleagues encouraged and inspired Joyce's writing during his university days. In 1900, his first work—a review of Henrik Ibsen's play *When We Dead Awaken*—was published in *The Fortnightly Review*. Inspired by Ibsen's work, Joyce wrote his own play shortly thereafter, entitled *A Brilliant Career*. He was unhappy with the finished product, however, and later destroyed it. Only the dedication page of the play still remains. It reads, "To My own Soul I dedicate the first true work of my life."

In November of 1901, Joyce wrote an article (titled *The Day of the Rabblement*), which criticized the Irish theatrical circle for avoiding producing works by the likes of Henrik Ibsen and Leo Tolstoy. Instead of looking outward and exploring more worldly content, he felt they merely produced performances that fostered "nostalgic Irish populism." University College refused to print the article because Joyce mentioned *Il fuoco*, a novel by Gabriele D'Annunzio which was banned by the Roman Catholic Church at the time.

With the help of his friend Francis Sheehy Skeffington, Joyce soon found a way around the university's refusal to print the article. Skeffington had also recently written an article the university rejected, and together, he and Joyce published their articles on their own and distributed them by hand.

A copy of the article landed on the desk of Arthur Griffith, who at the time owned and edited the newspaper *United Irishman*. Griffith himself would go on to do great things during the Irish War of Independence, including founding the Sinn Féin political party (still a major political party in Ireland today), and he was a key figure in the production and negotiation of the Anglo-Irish Treaty of 1921, which established the Free Irish State, now known as the Republic of Ireland. Griffith was so impressed by Joyce's work that he published an article in his newspaper criticizing the censorship by the university.

When Joyce graduated in October 1902, he—perhaps surprisingly—decided to study medicine. He attended several classes at the Catholic University Medical School in Dublin but eventually had to leave when they declined to provide him with a paid tutoring position to help him pay the tuition. Upon learning this, Joyce left Ireland and moved to Paris, where he was accepted at the École de Médecine to study physics, chemistry, and biology. During the months that followed, Joyce wrote home regularly to ask for money (which his family, no doubt, could not afford to send), as well as complain about the cold weather and the change in his diet, which he blamed for his constant poor health.

In late January of 1903, Joyce left school, though he remained in Paris for another few months until bad news brought him back home.

Chapter Three

Music, Poetry, and Love

"They lived and laughed and loved and left."

—James Joyce

In the spring of 1903, Joyce received word that his mother was ill and likely dying. He promptly returned to Dublin and began to care for her full-time. Joyce's father, John, had descended deeper into his drinking habits and turned abusive in the previous few years, which made tensions in the household run high. Nevertheless, Joyce spent most of his time at home with his mother, caring for her needs and reading aloud to her, mostly from his own writing and drafts he was working on. Most notably, he read several chapters that would eventually appear in his unfinished work, *Stephen Hero*.

In the days leading up to May's death on August 13, 1903, she urged her son to attend confession and take communion with her. By this time, however, Joyce's faith was all but nonexistent, and his mother died without having her request granted. In the days following her death, members of the family would kneel at her bedside and pray, but Joyce and his younger brother Stanislaus refused to do so. This may have been the straw that broke the camel's back of the already strained family, and from this point on, Joyce would spend less and less time at home and more with his old friends from school. To make ends meet, he started reviewing books for local newspapers and publications.

Less than a year later, Joyce met Nora Barnacle, a 21-year-old from Galway who had come to Dublin to find work. On June 16, 1904, they took a walk together through Ringsend, a suburb of Dublin, and during this date, Joyce had his first sexual encounter, which had a profound effect on him. In fact, the events of *Ulysses* begin on the same calendar day, and today, Bloomsday is celebrated in Ireland on June 16 every year to commemorate the life of Joyce and his works.

Not long after Joyce and Nora's first date, Joyce was out drinking with friends when he was assaulted by a man after Joyce approached the man's female companion. An old friend of

Joyce's father by the name of Alfred Hunter witnessed the event and helped Joyce to his home to get him cleaned up and treat his injuries. Hunter himself was subject to plenty of local gossip and rumors—it was said he was secretly a Jew and that his wife had long been unfaithful to him. It is perhaps this encounter, mixed with the air of mystery surrounding Hunter, that led Joyce to eventually use Hunter as a basis for Leopold Bloom, the main character of *Ulysses*.

Throughout 1904, Joyce pursued two goals: furthering his writing career and exploring the possibility of becoming a musician. Joyce had been a talented singer since childhood, perhaps due to his early commitment to the Catholic Church and the Sodality of Our Lady, which would have required boys to sing in the church choir.

In May, Joyce participated in a competition for all types of musicians, including singers. In preparation for the contest, he took extensive singing lessons with two separate instructors and even sold several books from his personal collection in order to pay the entry fee to the competition. The contest consisted of three rounds, where Joyce was expected to sing three different songs. He performed exceptionally in the first two rounds, but in the third round, he was told he would have to sight-read the song from sheet music. Unable to do this, he refused to participate in the third round. Despite this, Joyce placed third in the competition overall, and though he gave up the idea of a career as a musician after this, he continued to sing at various concerts around Dublin that year.

Around the same time, Joyce also submitted a piece of writing to the journal *Dana* entitled *A Portrait of the Artist*. The editor rejected it outright, stating, "I can't print what I can't understand." Instead of abandoning the work, Joyce reworked it into a fictional account of his childhood and added much of it to the unfinished manuscript he had read to his mother on her deathbed, *Stephen Hero*.

Joyce wrote several other pieces throughout the remainder of 1904, including a poem that was a parody of William Butler Yeats' work "To Ireland in the Coming Times." Joyce titled his own work "The Holy Office" and used it to criticize, again, Irish literary circles and their refusal to focus on a wider variety of writing. This poem was also rejected because it was, ironically, considered "unholy." Three of his poems did get published that year in various newspapers and journals, and three of his short stories were published in the *Irish Homestead*, a weekly publication that focused on Irish agriculture. These works eventually became the basis for Joyce's later, more extensive work called *Dubliners*.

In late 1904, Joyce moved into a property owned by his friend Oliver St. John Gogarty. He lasted less than a week, however, as one night Gogarty and another roommate, presumably drunk, fired a pistol inside the home and narrowly missed shooting Joyce in his bed. Longing for a change, Joyce and his girlfriend Nora borrowed money from several friends and acquaintances and subsequently left Ireland for mainland Europe.

Joyce always had a complex relationship with his homeland and would not return to live in Ireland again. He later wrote, "When the Irishman is found outside of Ireland in another environment, he very often becomes a respected man. The economic and intellectual conditions that prevail in his own country do not permit the development of individuality. . . . No one who has any self-respect stays in Ireland, but flees afar as though from a country that has undergone the visitation of an angered Jove." Yet although

James Joyce often rejected Ireland, he wrote of little else throughout his life.

Chapter Four

The Irish Exile

"Ireland is the old sow that eats her farrow."

—James Joyce

James and Nora took a few detours through London and Paris to secure more money before heading to Zürich, Switzerland, where Joyce had been led to believe there was a teaching vacancy at the Berlitz Language School. Unfortunately, he had been misinformed, and the couple remained in Zürich only for a little over a week. On another recommendation, they next headed to Trieste in northeastern Italy, which was then part of the Austro-Hungarian Empire. In a continuance of bad luck, there was no position available at the school there, either. The director of the school, perhaps seeing their desperation, instead secured a position for Joyce as an English teacher in Pola (in modern-day Croatia), a major naval base at the time.

It was during this same chaotic period that Nora became pregnant, which would have been a huge scandal in Ireland at the time since James and Nora were unmarried. Nevertheless, they became good friends with the director of the school in Pola and his wife, and Joyce continued to write between teaching. Apart from his new friends, however, Joyce never really liked the city, calling it "a naval Siberia." He left as soon as he could when he learned there was a new job available back in Trieste.

At age 23, Joyce took up teaching English at the Berlitz school in Trieste. When summer came, he finally began to feel financially stable and had his poem "Holy Office" (which had earlier been rejected for publication) self-published and distributed back in Dublin by his younger brother, Stanislaus. Nora meanwhile gave birth to their son Giorgio on July 27, 1905. Shortly after that, Stanislaus moved to Trieste and into the apartment that the family shared with another couple. Joyce secured him a position at the school where he taught, and the entire household pooled their income while Joyce continued to write.

A London publisher, Richard Grant, had agreed to publish Joyce's collection of short stories, *Dubliners*, and Joyce had finished all but one story when the publisher withdrew their agreement in 1906. More than a few passages within the work were considered controversial, and under British law at the time, the publisher could be held liable by the courts if they published works that contained indecent language. Despite several negotiations between the publisher and Joyce, which attempted to limit the legal liability of the publisher without sacrificing Joyce's artistic integrity, the publishing house held firm on their refusal to print the collection.

Chapter Five

Struggle to get Published

"Writing in English is the most ingenious torture ever devised for sins committed in previous lives."

—James Joyce

In the summer of 1906, the school where Joyce was employed ran into financial difficulties after the head of the school embezzled a huge sum of the funds and absconded with them. The new director could only afford to keep one of the Joyce brothers employed, and the elder Joyce, discouraged by his inability to get *Dubliners* published, decided to leave Trieste after securing a position as a clerk at a bank in Rome.

In Joyce's personal correspondence, he admits that he felt extremely unproductive during the seven months he spent in Rome, though history would say he accomplished plenty. He further revised *Dubliners* and even came up with the idea for the final story in the collection, titled "The Dead." He decided here to convert *Ulysses*, which was only a collection of notes and ideas at this time, from a short story as he originally planned into a full-length novel. Rome also served as the inspiration for his only extant play, *Exiles*, which he would finish and publish later when he returned to Trieste. Finally, during this brief period in Rome, Joyce was exposed to many socialist writings, which would later influence the character of Leopold Bloom in *Ulysses*.

Several of his poems were published in London during this time in a collection titled *Chamber Music*, but Joyce was still financially strained, overworked, and unhappy in his job, which took up almost all of his time. He returned to Trieste after seven months when he found out that Nora was pregnant again with their second child. In Trieste, he struggled to find full-time work but gave private English lessons and filled in at the Berlitz school when the opportunity arose. A few of his private students not only influenced his ongoing writings but helped him get published.

Italo Svevo, an Italian author, was one of Joyce's students, and Joyce learned extensively about Judaism from him. Judaism was something he had only been previously exposed to through rumors (such as those surrounding Alfred Hunter) and in some of the socialist writings he had encountered while in Rome. Leopold Bloom would continue to take shape as Joyce began to fold some of Svevo's views into the character, which was still only a few jotted notes here and there. Svevo almost served as a support system for Joyce's writing, as he encouraged him through a bout of writer's block with *A Portrait of the Artist as a Young Man.*

Another student of Joyce's was Roberto Prezioso, the editor of a major Italian newspaper. Joyce wrote several articles for the newspaper focused on and directed toward separatists in Trieste who sought independence from the Austro-Hungarian Empire and a return to Italian sovereignty. Joyce compared the struggles of these separatists to those of the Irish in their struggle to obtain independence from Great Britain. The articles led to him being invited to speak at Trieste's local university, where he gave several lectures both on Ireland and the arts.

That summer, Joyce became ill with what is believed to have been rheumatic fever, which causes inflammation of the heart, blood vessels, and joints. He developed eyesight problems during the course of the illness and was unable to work for several weeks, though he finally managed to finish "The Dead," which had taken shape back in Rome and served as the final story in *Dubliners*. While he was struggling with this illness, his daughter Lucia was born on July 26, 1907.

Over the following year, Joyce took extensive notes of his observations of the people and places in Trieste to help him create the characters of Leopold and Molly Bloom. These notes would form the basis for what would later become *Ulysses*. It was also during this period that he reworked large portions of *Stephen Hero* into his later published work *A Portrait of the Artist as a Young Man*.

By July of 1909, Joyce was blessed with a sudden infusion of money when a private tutoring student paid him for lessons for a year in advance. He used the funds and the opportunity to return to Ireland briefly to introduce his son to his family in Dublin. While in Ireland, he applied for a position in the Italian language department at his old school but was not offered the job. He also had several meetings with an Irish publisher, George Roberts of Maunsel and Company, who was interested in *Dubliners*. No final decisions were made during this trip, and negotiations would continue for several years. Two months later, he returned to Trieste and brought one of his younger sisters, Eva, who would help Nora with the children and the home. She would return to Ireland after less than two years, citing homesickness.

Joyce was only home in Trieste for a month before he formed an idea for a business venture: opening a cinema in Dublin. At the time, there were several cinemas in Trieste but none in Dublin, and Joyce was sure it would be a financial success. He garnered funds from several local investors in Trieste, and by October, he had launched Ireland's first cinema, the Volta on Mary Street, which was remarkably well-received. Unfortunately, shortly after Joyce returned to Trieste in January of 1910 (with his sister Eileen in tow), the cinema quickly declined and eventually closed. Eileen would remain in mainland Europe (unlike Eva) and eventually married a Czech banker.

In the following two years, Joyce had no financial stability to speak of, which caused further tensions between his family members. He consistently depended on his brother Stanislaus to loan him money to support Nora, his children, and his sisters Eva and Eileen; because of this, his relationship with his brother eventually broke down. To make ends meet, he lectured several more times at the local university and even applied to the University of Padua to obtain a teaching certificate in English, but his application was rejected because the university did not recognize his Irish diploma.

Joyce returned to Dublin briefly with his family in the summer of 1912 to solidify the publication of *Dubliners*, but the negotiations came to nothing. The publisher, George Roberts, was concerned with legal liabilities, so after three years of back-and-forth, *Dubliners* was refused publication a second time. Disappointed, Joyce returned to Trieste; he would never see his homeland again.

Chapter Six

The Artist and the Great War

"Whoever has the last sack of flour will win the war."

—James Joyce

Joyce was initially furious about *Dubliners'* continued failure to get published, and in a fit of rage, he threw his drafts of *A Portrait of the Artist of a Young Man* into the fire. It was rescued by what friends of Joyce's would later call a "family fire brigade," most notably his partner, Nora, and his sister, Eileen.

Fortunately, Joyce did not have much more time to feel discouraged; in 1913, he received news that changed the tide of his fortune. Richard Grant, the original London publisher to whom he had first pitched the collection, re-established contact and agreed, at last, to produce the work. Nearly nine years after Joyce had originally submitted the manuscript to Grant, *Dubliners* was finally published in June 1914.

This collection of fifteen short stories focuses on the lives of middle-class Irish in Dublin at the turn of the twentieth century. Much of Joyce's earlier writing was a critique of Irish nationalism, and *Dubliners* was a deeper exploration of this, questioning how Ireland could, in essence, find itself and develop its own identity set apart from British colonialism. "My intention," said Joyce, "was to write a chapter of the moral history of my country, and I chose Dublin for the scene because that city seemed to me the center of paralysis."

Each story is told from the perspective of a single individual at a specific stage in their life. The earlier stories are from the viewpoints of children, while later stories have progressively older protagonists. The collection is often divided into three acts for childhood, adolescence, and maturity. Each story centers on a single moment in the character's life where they have a moment of enlightenment. It was through these moments that Joyce urged the Irish people to develop their own identities, which he believed was the first step to Ireland's spiritual liberation, if not its sovereign one.

It was perhaps through the publishing of this work that Joyce came to the attention of Ezra Pound, an American poet and literary critic living in London. Pound established contact with Joyce and would play a major role in encouraging Joyce's writing and aiding him in the publication of his work, as well as its promotion in literary circles and to the general public. Pound first included one of the poems from Joyce's *Chàmber Music* in an anthology journal for which he was editor, *Des Imagistes*. When Joyce finally completed *A Portrait of the Artist as a Young Man* in 1914, Pound was instrumental in its publication in the London literary magazine *The Egoist*.

The dawn of the First World War in August of 1914 would not change much for Joyce and his family at first. Despite the fact that they were citizens of the United Kingdom, which was now at war with Austria-Hungary (of which Trieste was the fourth-largest city at that time), they stayed for nearly another year in Trieste. This was even after Stanislaus, Joyce's younger brother, was interned for publicly declaring his sympathies for local separatist groups. It was only in May of 1915, when Italy declared war on Austria-Hungary, that Joyce and his family fled.

Considering Joyce's background, crossing a border was not necessarily a simple task, especially in wartime. Joyce was Irish but held a British passport. Political tensions between Irish separatists and British loyalists were heating up even despite the larger international conflicts of World War I, essentially placing a target on Joyce's back as he attempted to flee the war. Furthermore, he was a resident of Trieste, which was now in upheaval after Italy declared its intentions to join the war front.

Joyce had to sign a parole agreement with Austria-Hungary in order to leave its borders, essentially promising he would not enlist in any military force that opposed their goals. With barely more than the clothes on their backs, he and his family absconded to neutral Switzerland and the city of Zürich. For the duration of the war, both British and Austro-Hungarian intelligence agencies kept the family under surveillance.

Now that they were clear of any potential violence, Joyce was back in a familiar situation: broke, with no income to speak of, and a domestic partner and two children to support. *A Portrait of the Artist as a Young Man* had not yet made its debut appearance in *The Egoist*, and *Dubliners* had only been (at last) published a mere two weeks before Archduke Franz Ferdinand had been assassinated and the Great War had begun. By the end of 1914, *Dubliners* had only sold 499 copies, 120 of which Joyce had been required to buy himself. In the first six months of 1915, it sold another twenty-six copies, and an additional seven copies were sold in the second half of that year. Reading for pleasure was a luxury few could afford at this time, and the works of a heretofore unknown writer were of low priority.

It was only through friends and supporters that Joyce was able to survive financially throughout the duration of World War I. His advocate in London, Ezra Pound, along with poet William Butler Yeats (whom Joyce had once parodied in his poetry), petitioned the British government to use the Royal Literary Fund to provide Joyce with a stipend. In addition, the editor of *The Egoist* (which would soon begin its serial publication of *A Portrait of the Artist as a Young Man*) would also send him considerable financial aid throughout this time, and continued throughout the rest of his life.

Thanks to such generous donations, Joyce and his family were able to live more comfortably than they ever had before, a situation that would continue through the end of 1918. Bolstered by this support on multiple fronts, Joyce began to dedicate more and more of his time to writing. In 1915, he completed his play *Exiles* and finally began the first draft of *Ulysses*, which up to that point had only been a series of ideas, notes, and outlines. He also began work on a new piece he titled *Giacomo Joyce* but abandoned it in favor of other, more robust works.

Chapter Seven

Zürich: An Artistic Haven

"I will try to express myself in some mode of life or art as freely as I can, using for my defense the only arms I allow myself to use—silence, exile and cunning."

—James Joyce

Zürich was a popular destination for artists of all kinds during the war, and Joyce took full advantage of this. He spent significant time at local cafes, conversing with artists from all over greater Europe, making observations, and taking notes to incorporate into his works-in-progress. He was introduced to Dadaism through the local Cabaret Voltaire, an avant-garde art style that criticized the obsession with the aesthetics of modern capitalist society.

His play, *Exiles*, would premiere in Munich in 1919, thanks to Stefan Zweig, an Austrian writer he met in Zürich during this time. He also re-established his interest in music through connections to expatriate musicians and even took lessons. Much of what he learned about musical notation in this period made its way, eventually, into the pages of *Ulysses*.

In April of 1916, in the midst of the Great War, a violent insurrection occurred in Ireland. The Easter Rising (named so because it began on Easter Sunday) lasted for six days, with the goal of gaining independence from Great Britain and establishing the Irish Free State. It ended in mostly civilian casualties and the unconditional surrender of the Irish rebel forces. Sixteen of the leaders of the insurrection were publicly executed, and counted among the dead was one of Joyce's closest friends from his university days—Francis Sheehy Skeffington.

Skeffington had previously expressed his support of the Irish Volunteers, but as they became more violent, his concerns grew. During the Easter Rising, he publicly begged the people of Dublin to avoid looting during the violence. He was subsequently arrested (most likely because police thought he was part of the uprising) and unceremoniously taken out of his cell and shot in the prison yard.

Joyce was publicly tight-lipped about both the Easter Rising and the greater World War, maintaining an image of neutrality throughout the duration of the conflicts. He toed a delicate line when he did speak on the events unfolding in Ireland, saying that while he agreed with the creation of an independent Irish state, he did not condone the violent methods that were now being used to reach that goal. Instead of getting mired down in politics (which would have been very easy at this time), he remained focused on his writing, *Ulysses* in particular.

Thanks to their newfound financial stability, Joyce and his family often went to stay in Locarno, an Italian-speaking region of Switzerland. Initially, the family went there to seek medical attention for both Joyce himself and his partner Nora, both of whom were stricken with multiple illnesses during their time in Switzerland. Nora reportedly had several nervous breakdowns, though the true nature of her illnesses has never been confirmed.

Joyce, on the other hand, had numerous compounding issues with his eyes, which had begun during his bout of rheumatic fever back in 1907. In 1917, he wrote to Ezra Pound regarding the issue, "On Saturday when walking in the street I got suddenly a violent Hexenschuss which incapacitated me from moving for about twenty minutes. I managed to crawl into a tram and get home. It got better in the evening but next day I had symptoms of glaucoma again—slightly better today. Tomorrow morning I am going to the Augenklinik. This climate is impossible for me so that, operated or not, I want to go away next month. I am advised to go to Italian Switzerland."

Joyce had developed glaucoma, and it was in Locarno that he had the first of what would become eleven surgeries on his eyes in an attempt to save his vision. Even though the issues with his eyes continued, they still worked, and Joyce engaged in several affairs during this period. The first was with Gertrude Kaempffer, a 26-year-old woman recovering from tuberculosis in a town adjacent to Locarno. While she declined a physical relationship when Joyce attempted to initiate one, they did engage in a lengthy affair comprised of erotic letters, which Joyce managed to hide from Nora by instructing Gertrude to send the letter *poste restante*—an order that indicated the letter should be held at the post office for pickup by the recipient, rather than delivered directly to their home. In *Ulysses*, protagonist Leopold Bloom does the same with a lover.

His second affair occurred back in Zürich with a neighbor named Marthe Fleischmann. Their homes were close enough to each other that they could see through the other's windows, and Joyce caught sight of her first as she was pulling a toilet chain to flush. This was the inspiration for a particular quirk he gave to his protagonist in his later novel *Finnegans Wake,* who has a predilection to watching attractive women urinate. They first began their affair, as Joyce did with Gertrude, by writing letters. A few months later, Joyce borrowed a friend's apartment for the evening and consummated the affair, telling his friend later that he had "explored the coldest and hottest parts of a woman's body."

Even in spite of his worsening eyes, Joyce also made plenty of artistic progress, though that progress was not without its setbacks. In 1914, *A Portrait of the Artist as a Young Man* began to circulate in *The Egoist.* This novel follows protagonist Stephen Daedalus as he undergoes a spiritual and intellectual awakening. Joyce made it no secret that Daedalus was his own fictional alter-ego, and *A Portrait of the Artist as a Young Man* was a semi-fictional autobiography. Throughout the five chapters of the novel, Daedalus explores elements of Catholicism and

Irish culture, and how they are inextricably linked. He becomes critical of Catholic doctrine and the cultural conventions of the average Irish person and eventually exiles himself in Ireland to live out the rest of his life in Europe.

While *A Portrait of the Artist as a Young Man* had finally begun to print in *The Egoist*, some of the serial chapters had been censored by the printers. This was frustrating for Joyce, as he valued his artistic integrity, and he eventually found someone who was willing to publish the work in full—and uncensored—in 1916. With the continued help of Ezra Pound, he was also able to obtain a commitment to publish *Ulysses* in serial format in *The Little Review*, an American literary magazine.

Joyce also entered the world of theater during the war, as he co-founded the English Players, a company of actors that the British government eventually endorsed and helped fund as a contribution to the war effort. They staged plays written primarily by Irish playwrights and employed local actors and other artists. Joyce was the business manager and had planned to put up his own play, *Exiles*, but the Influenza Pandemic of 1918 put a temporary halt to public productions, and Joyce moved on to other things.

When World War I ended in 1918, so too did much of Joyce's financial support. Zürich was not a cheap place to live, and the income from his published work alone was not enough to support himself and his family. The city also began to grow quite lonely for Joyce as many of his artistic colleagues moved back to their home countries.

In October of 1919, Joyce and his family returned to Trieste, but it was not the same Trieste they had left four years ago. No longer part of the now-defunct Austro-Hungarian Empire, Trieste was now simply another Italian city devastated by the war. Knowing he could not stay there, Joyce collaborated with Ezra Pound on his next move, and in June 1920, he made Paris his new home.

Chapter Eight

The Odyssey Ends as Ulysses Begins

"The supreme question about a work of art is out of how deep a life does it spring."

—James Joyce

Joyce's first four months in Paris were about making connections with the goal of eventually moving on to London. Ezra Pound once again came to Joyce's rescue and set up introductions to initiate him into the literary and artistic circles of Paris. It was there Joyce met Sylvia Beach, who would provide financial support in the future, as well as become a publisher of his works. She ran Shakespeare and Company, a bookshop on the Rive Gauche in Paris.

The Little Review in New York had begun to publish *Ulysses* in serial format in March of 1918, even though Joyce would not finish the complete work until 1921. He was now struggling to find someone willing to publish it as a novel, but that would become the least of his issues in short order. Two installments of *Ulysses* in 1919 had been suppressed from publication, as they had been cited as "obscene" and "potentially subversive." This was exacerbated further when an unknown person mailed a yet unpublished installment to a lawyer in New York who was part of the New York Society for the Suppression of Vice, which filed an official complaint against *Ulysses* and Joyce.

The complaint led to a trial, where the publishers were each fined $50, the equivalent of over $800 today. They were also ordered to cease publication of any future installments immediately. The outcome of the trial scared off the American publisher who was considering publishing *Ulysses* in full. The ripple effect scared off potential British publishers as well, and eventually, the novel was banned outright in the United Kingdom in 1922. The ban would not be lifted until 1936.

Understandably, the trial and its outcome generated a massive amount of free publicity for the book, which was no longer available. Sylvia Beach of Shakespeare and Company would be Joyce's saving grace, as she agreed to publish

Ulysses independently through her bookshop. A pre-order list began to form of interested readers both in Europe and the United States, and Beach shipped copies as they were printed.

When the dissemination of the book, and the method of doing so, came to the attention of authorities, the postal services of both France and the U.K. began checking packages and confiscating any copies of the book. This only added fuel to the fire, and the book began to be smuggled to interested readers. In the United States, since the book had no copyright (due to the ban), pirated copies were published and sold. *Ulysses* was only legally sold in the United States after a 1934 lawsuit, *United States v. One Book Called Ulysses*, in which the judge ruled that the book was not obscene and lifted the ban.

Ulysses is considered one of the greatest works of modernist literature of all time. It is based loosely on Homer's Greek epic the *Odyssey* and even takes its name from the Latinized name of the *Odyssey's* titular hero, Odysseus. The events of the novel take place over the course of a single day and are largely composed of the inner thoughts and feelings of its cast of characters. It is one of the first—and largely considered to be the best—works to use stream-of-consciousness writing, as it flawlessly imitates the true inner dialogue of an individual in their day-to-day lives.

The book is divided into eighteen parts, with each one playing out over the course of approximately one hour. It is considered a remarkably accurate depiction of Dublin at the dawn of the twentieth century, focusing on the poverty and squalor of the city. Joyce drew these details from his own memory, the recollections of friends and colleagues, and his own nearly obsessive reading of *Thom's Directory*, an annually revised almanac that listed every property in the city (both residential and commercial) and the property's owners.

Many of the critics of the book, which helped lead to the original ban, considered it obscene due to the sexual nature of several parts of the novel, but Joyce's mastery of metaphorical language is what led to the ban being overturned, as a judge ruled that the language was not explicit enough to be considered pornographic.

Chapter Nine

Family Troubles

"Jesus was a bachelor and never lived with a woman. Surely living with a woman is one of the most difficult things a man has to do, and he never did it."

—James Joyce

With *Ulysses* being printed regardless of bans and with all of his ongoing works now finally complete, Joyce turned his attention to what would come next. He began toying with an experimental novel in 1923 that he first called *Work in Progress* but would eventually, 16 years later, become *Finnegans Wake*. Even before the work was complete, Joyce had found a publisher willing to serialize the novel for their magazine called *Transition*. Joyce likely had a much easier time finding a publisher thanks to the buzz surrounding *Ulysses*.

Unfortunately, despite Joyce's growing professional literary popularity and acclaim, his health continued to decline. While in Paris, he underwent almost a dozen eye surgeries to relieve the pain and symptoms of glaucoma, but his vision continued to worsen regardless. By 1930, all of his teeth had been removed due to repeated infections following surgery, and he was blind in his left eye, with his right eye not faring much better. He needed two magnifying glasses to read and, more importantly, to write. He feared he would never finish *Finnegans Wake* and asked fellow Irish author James Stephens to finish the novel if he himself could not. Fortunately, this would turn out to be unnecessary.

Joyce's visual limitations did not stop him from enjoying the fame and fortune he had finally acquired. His royalties gave him a steady stream of income, and his other investments continued to make regular returns. Perhaps he inherited the trait from his father John, but Joyce was known to be remarkably bad at money management and often lived beyond his means. All the while, he managed to continue to write.

Finnegans Wake would not, however, receive the same controversial but warm reception as *Ulysses* had. While the book also used a stream-of-consciousness style and made heavy use of literary allusions, Joyce pushed them to an extreme, which made the writing difficult to understand. Much of the book is also written in obscure or archaic English, further alienating the casual reader. It is also remarkably nonlinear and can be read by opening the complete work to any single page. Upon reading some of the first installments, even some of Joyce's strongest supporters reacted negatively and criticized the work. Among them were his own brother, Stanislaus, and his longtime advocate Ezra Pound.

Rather than being discouraged by this, Joyce worked with the editors of *Transition* to put together a collection of essays from various literary voices who praised *Finnegans Wake*. Contributing authors included Samuel Beckett, an Irish novelist who idolized Joyce and would go on to become one of the last great modernist writers, and William Carlos Williams, a respected American poet. The publication of this collection managed to stir up interest from the general public after the initial harsh reviews, and with the help of American poet and playwright T. S. Eliot, *Finnegans Wake* would finally be published in London in 1939.

It was several years earlier, in 1930, that Joyce began thinking of his legacy. His son

Giorgio had just married, but Joyce and Nora still remained unwed, which could create potential complications with Giorgio's inheritance according to British law. In order to secure this, Joyce moved back to London to establish residency there. He registered to vote and through proper channels rented a long-term residence. On July 4, 1931, after 27 years together, Joyce and Nora finally got married in the eyes of the law. They remained in London for another six months to fulfill their residency requirements but then left on short notice when they received bad news from Paris. Their daughter, Lucia, was ill.

Lucia Joyce had made her own name for herself, separate from her father, as a promising dancer. She studied under some of the biggest names at the time, including Margaret Morris, Raymond Duncan, and Jean Borlin. In a review of one of her performances, a journalist of the *Paris Times* wrote: "Lucia Joyce is her father's daughter. She has James Joyce's enthusiasm, energy, and a not-yet-determined amount of his genius. When she reaches her full capacity for rhythmic dancing, James Joyce may yet be known as his daughter's father."

Shortly before she abruptly gave up dancing at the age of 22, Lucia engaged in a brief affair with Samuel Beckett, the same young writer who idolized her father's writing. She was said to be head-over-heels in love, but the relationship was short and ill-fated. Beckett was seeing other women at the time, and it wasn't long before he admitted to Lucia that he was not actually interested in her and was essentially using her to get closer to his hero, her father. It is unclear if Joyce himself was aware of this or if it had any bearing on Lucia quitting a promising dance career just as it was beginning.

Lucia began to exhibit signs of mental illness at this time. She engaged in several illicit affairs, and her behavior became increasingly erratic. In 1934, Joyce, concerned by her deteriorating mental state, took her to psychologist Carl Jung, who he knew casually through one of his former patrons. Jung, who had read *Ulysses* and compared it to the writing of a schizophrenic, diagnosed Lucia as such. She spent the next several years in and out of treatment in France, Switzerland, and the U.K.

While she was receiving treatment at St. Andrew's Hospital, Lucia insisted that she wanted to return to Paris, but doctors advised against it. They asked Joyce to sign papers to have her involuntarily committed, but Joyce refused, telling friends later that he would never agree to his daughter being "incarcerated among the English." Unfortunately, that is exactly what happened after Joyce's death, and Lucia remained institutionalized until her own death in 1982.

Throughout the 1930s, Joyce focused on his health and his family life. He based himself in Paris but made frequent trips to Switzerland for surgeries and treatment on his eyes, as well as treatment for Lucia. When the end of the decade approached, the stage was set for another world war to begin, and Joyce was vocal about his opposition to fascism. Throughout his life, he had taken an interest in the Jewish plight, and he was horrified at the growing anti-semitic sentiments throughout Europe.

Even before World War II officially began, Joyce was directly involved in helping at least 16 Jewish individuals escape persecution. These activities only came to an end in 1940, when Paris was officially occupied by Hitler's forces. Joyce and his family were forced to leave France immediately and sought refuge back in Zürich.

Chapter Ten

An Icon's Death, a Legacy Left

"When I die, Dublin will be written on my heart."

—James Joyce

Though Joyce and his family had lived in Zürich for the duration of World War I and for a time after, they had considerable trouble entering Switzerland in 1940. The family sought temporary refuge with the publishers of *Finnegans Wake* while Joyce applied to the Swiss government for visas. Their application was rejected on the assumption that Joyce, his wife, and his children were Jews.

While Switzerland did grant refugee status to approximately 25,000 Jews through the duration of the war, they also denied entry to over 30,000. Historians have debated the political and economic reasons for this, but it is largely agreed that Switzerland, as a neutral party in the war with little to no military to speak of, was not in a position to open its borders to all refugees without risking direct invasion from German forces in retaliation.

Joyce himself pleaded with the Swiss Alien Police on the matter, declaring in private that he "was not a Jew from Judea but an Aryan from Erin." Several of Joyce's friends, including Swiss writer Jacques Mercanton and the mayor of Zürich himself, personally vouched for Joyce, and his family was eventually granted visas after paying a guarantee of 20,000 Swiss francs.

After entering Switzerland on December 14, 1940, they spent the night at the Richemonde Hotel, where they met Sean Lester, the secretary-general of the League of Nations and a fellow Irishman from Belfast. He took tea with the Joyces and asked why they had chosen to come to Switzerland. "They said that Zürich had always been associated with certain crises in their life," Lester later recounted. "They had spent their honeymoon there; it was there that Joyce's eyesight had been saved and now they were going back in another crisis. They liked the solid virtues of the people."

When they arrived in Zürich, Joyce took it upon himself to write a letter to the mayor, to thank him for his help in entering the country. He said, "The connection between me and your hospitable city extends over a period of nearly forty years and in these painful times I feel honoured that I should owe my presence here in large part to the personal guaranty of Zürich's first citizen." Sadly, Joyce would not have much time to enjoy his return to Switzerland.

Nearly a month later, on January 11, 1941, Joyce went into surgery to address a perforated ulcer, which was causing severe abdominal pain. The surgery seemed to go well, but the next day, Joyce suddenly fell into a coma for just over 24 hours. On January 13, he suddenly awakened around two in the morning and asked a nurse to call his wife and son so he could see them. Fifteen minutes later, while Nora and Giorgio were still on their way, James Joyce died. He was 59 years old.

His funeral was small, attended by his wife, his son and family, a friend of Joyce's who sang at the burial service, and the British consul in Switzerland. Two Irish diplomats were in Switzerland at the time of Joyce's death, but they declined to attend. When the Irish government was informed of his death by Swiss authorities, they merely asked if he had died a Catholic.

Ironically, a Catholic priest had offered to perform the service for Joyce's burial, but Nora declined, stating, "I couldn't do that to him."

Several years later, the Irish government denied Nora's petition to have her husband's remains repatriated to his homeland. He remains buried in an honor grave at Fluntern Cemetery in Zürich. Every year on June 16, Bloomsday, his life is celebrated in countries all over the world. Those who wish to honor him make the trek to Switzerland to pay their respects and read aloud his works at his gravesite, keeping his monumental legacy alive.

Conclusion

James Joyce's work has had an undeniable effect on literary culture, both in Ireland and around the world. Modern-day writers study his work, particularly *Ulysses*, for its unconventional and revolutionary use of language. Joyce's ability to focus on the minutiae of everyday life and make it something profound and beautiful is an enviable talent to writers the world over and something that paved the way for future artists to explore these intricacies in a variety of mediums in the years following his death.

His works frequently appear on lists of "Must Read" books, as his unique style continues to elicit new interpretations of each allusion and metaphor, each turn of phrase. Scholars dedicate their careers to exploring his body of work, which is minuscule in the grand scheme of things: only three novels, one collection of short stories, a single play, and two books of poetry. Still, there have been over 15,000 pieces of media written about him, whether it be articles, theses, new editions and translations, and so on. The people he inspired within his lifetime went on to shape literary discourse for a generation.

Perhaps James Joyce said it best when he quipped, "I've put in so many enigmas and puzzles that it will keep the professors busy for centuries arguing over what I meant, and that is the only way of ensuring one's immortality."

Bibliography

Beja, Morris (1992). *James Joyce: A Literary Life*.

Bowker, Gordon (2012). *James Joyce: A New Biography*.

Ellmann, Richard (1982). *James Joyce*.

Fairhall, James (1993). *James Joyce and the Question of History*.

Shloss, Carol Loeb (2005). *Lucia Joyce: To Dance in the Wake*.

Vanderham, Paul (1997). *James Joyce and Censorship: The Trials of Ulysses*.

Made in the USA
Columbia, SC
14 December 2022